THE FAMILY
OF CATS

THE FAMILY
OF CATS

Illustrations by Joseph Wolf

AMERICAN MUSEUM OF NATURAL HISTORY • NEW YORK

POMEGRANATE ARTBOOKS • SAN FRANCISCO

Published by Pomegranate Artbooks
Box 6099, Rohnert Park, California 94927

Pomegranate Europe Ltd.
Fullbridge House, Fullbridge
Maldon, Essex CM9 7LE, England

ISBN 0-7649-0335-7
Pomegranate Catalog No. A882

Designed by Bonnie Smetts Design

Printed in Hong Kong
01 00 99 98 97 96   6 5 4 3 2 1

First Edition

Introduction

D aniel Giraud Elliot (1835–1915), a wealthy New York naturalist, is credited with organizing the American Museum of Natural History Departments of Ornithology and Mammalogy. A founder of the American Ornithologists' Union (1883) and author of numerous scientific treatises, Elliot was also an accomplished artist who illustrated many of his works with his own fine drawings and watercolors. But for his great bird monographs and for *A monograph of the Felidae,* Dr. Elliot chose the finest natural history artist of the time, Joseph Wolf (1820–1899).

Joseph Wolf was born in the farming community of Moërz, Germany. As a young boy he loved to wander through the fields and woods and at an early age began sketching local animals and birds. At sixteen Joseph left his father's farm and went to work as an apprentice to a lithographer in Coblenz. Soon after he moved to Frankfurt, where he won commissions to illustrate major ornithological works by the eminent naturalists Edward Rüppell and Herman Schlegel. It was during this period that he received artistic training at the Antwerp Academy.

In 1848 Wolf moved to London at the invitation of D. W. Mitchell, Secretary of the Zoological Society of London. Wolf's excellent drawings of birds soon brought him to the attention of British naturalists and Sir Edward Landseer, the nature painter. Landseer sponsored Wolf's first submission of a painting to the Royal Academy, which helped to increase his commissions. Wolf supplied illustrations for both *The Proceedings of the Zoological Society of London* and *Transactions of the Zoological Society*, as well as for many important natural history monographs of the time. He was determined to be more than just a scientific draftsman, and he delighted in special commissions, such as painting Queen Victoria's pet bullfinch as a birthday gift from Princess Louise and the Marquis of Lorne.

Wolf spent considerable time sketching at the London Zoo, at private menageries, and in museum collections. He studied animals in the field and arranged his trips and vacations to enable him to observe birds and mammals in their natural environments. He filled a notebook with minute observations, body measurements, color of pelage and plumage, and behavior. He asserted that "we see distinctly only what we know thoroughly." It is this scholarly knowledge coupled with his extraordinary talent that made Joseph Wolf the preeminent illustrator of birds and mammals of the nineteenth century.

Daniel Giraud Elliot and Joseph Wolf formed a happy collaboration on five spectacular elephant folio atlases: *A monograph of the Tetraoninae, or family of the grouse* (1864–1865) and *The new and heretofore unfigured species of the birds of North America* (1866–1869), for which both men supplied illustrations; *A monograph of the Phasianidae, or family of the pheasants*

(1870–1872); *A monograph of the Paradiseidae, or the birds of paradise* (1873), illustrated by Wolf; and *A monograph of the Felidae, or family of cats* (1883), for which the artist drew 160 designs, of which 43 were published. Wolf was happiest and at his best when he was painting in browns and umbers; thus the big cats were especially to his liking. Elliot, in his introduction to the monograph, explains that he traveled to the great museums of Europe and America to examine collections of cats, especially type specimens, and to major zoos to study live animals. He reread the not inconsiderable literature, reviewed and revised the systematics of the *Felidae,* and then wrote his text.

From the information and sketches provided by Elliot, his own observations and sketches in the London Zoo, and skeletons, skins, and specimens in museums, Wolf was able to render the lions, panthers, and leopards in natural postures and habitats without ever having seen the particular species. A. H. Palmer, Wolf's biographer, wrote in 1895 that the cats' "beautiful coats and mighty muscles bring into play the artist's rare power of modeling, of foreshort-ening, and placing in faultless perspective the various markings." It is certain that Wolf never saw a Bengal leop-ard being sassed by a squirrel in a tree, a jaguarundi play-ing with an armadillo, or a Canadian lynx hunting a bird in the dead of winter. His ability to interpret scientific de-scriptions and to incorporate his study of big cat anatomy, musculature, movement, and coloration and his extraordi-nary imagination and artistic genius combined to produce the beautiful lifelike plates to illustrate Elliot's text.

A perfectionist, Wolf oversaw the lithography that had been entrusted to Joseph Smit (1836–1929), a Dutch zoological illustrator. When Smit came to London, Wolf befriended the young fellow foreigner. After working together on several projects, the two remained close friends until Wolf's death. During the production of the *Felidae*, Dr. Elliot would take his friend by cab from his Primrose Hill home near the London Zoo to the lithographer's residence so that Wolf could correct and approve the drawings translated by Smit onto stone. The images were then printed on fine folio-sized paper, and each copy was hand colored with watercolors under Smit's and, occasionally, Wolf's supervision, using Wolf's original watercolors as the standard.

Elliot wrote in 1872 that he was "sure that all naturalists will join me in acknowledging that Mr. Wolf is the only one who has succeeded in elevating to its proper position in art both ornithological and mammalogical illustration"—high praise indeed from a talented artist and demanding naturalist. And in the preface to the *Felidae*, Elliot wrote: "It is quite unnecessary for me to call attention to the Plates which ornament this volume. They are worthy of the great artist who produced them and they bear an enhanced value from the fact that they constitute the last series of drawings from my friend's magical pencil that will be devoted to scientific illustration."

Joseph Wolf had rheumatism that affected his arm, and eventually he could no longer undertake large projects, although he continued to sketch and paint for his own enjoyment. A perennial bachelor with many friends, he died quietly among his pet birds on April 20, 1899. Daniel Giraud Elliot outlived his friend and died of pneumonia in 1916; Joseph Smit died peacefully at age ninety-three.

In 1887 the Research Library of the American Museum of Natural History purchased Daniel Giraud Elliot's extensive library, including his great folio works and many of Joseph Wolf's elegant original watercolors and washes for these atlases. Among the collection are sixteen watercolors and twelve washes from the *Felidae* signed and dated by Wolf. These are counted among the Library's treasures.

—*Nina J. Root*

THE FAMILY
OF CATS

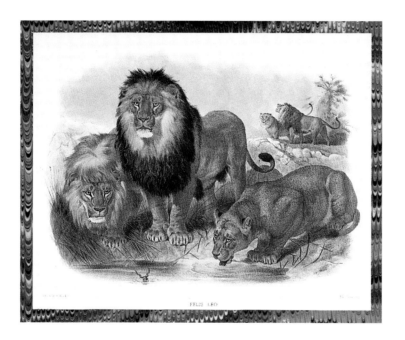

FELIS LEO

FELIS CONCOLOR.

FELIS TIGRIS.

FELIS UNCIA

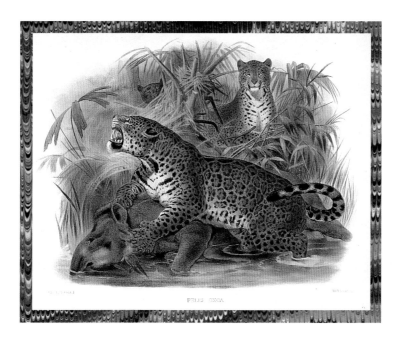

FELIS ONCA

FELIS PARDUS.

FELIS LEOPARDUS

FELIS DIARDI

FELIS MARMORATA

FELIS MANUL.

FELIS PAJEROS.

FELIS COLOCOLLA.

FELIS JAGUARONDI

FELIS CONCOLOR

FELIS BADIA

FEL'S TEMMINCKII

FELIS PLANICEPS.

FELIS TIGRINA

FELIS GEOFFROYI

FELIS BENGALENSIS

FELIS VIVERRINA

FELIS TRISTIS

FELIS SCRIPTA

FELIS CHRYSOTHRIX.

FELIS SERVAL

FELIS EUPTILURA.

1 no. F CHINENSIS   2 no. F SUMATRANA

FELIS JAVANENSIS

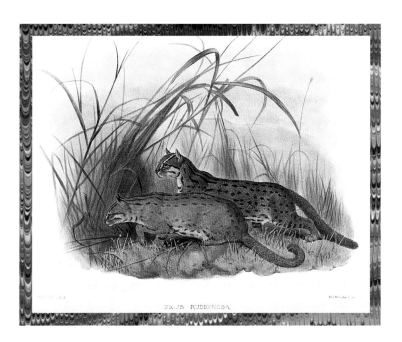

FELIS RUBIGINOSA.

FELIS CATUS

FELIS CAFFRA.

FELIS ORNATA.

FELIS CHAUS.

FELIS CAUDATUS

FELIS SHAWIANA

FELIS CERVARIA.

FELIS CANADENSIS

FELIS PARDINA.

FELIS LYNX.

FELIS RUFA

FELIS CARACAL.

FELIS DOMESTICA

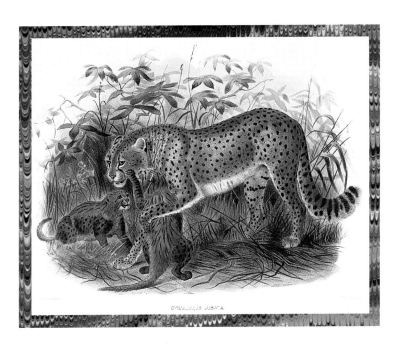

CYNAELURUS JUBATA

Illustrations

The Family of Cats

Compiled by Clare Flemming, Department of Mammalogy, American Museum of Natural History

Each entry below gives first the scientific name for the cat as given on the plate and the common name in use at that time, then the scientific and common names by which that mammal is known today.

Page 15
Felis leo
Lion
Now *Panthera leo*
Lion

Page 16
Felis concolor
Cougar, Puma, Panther, American Lion
Now *Puma concolor*
Puma, Panther, Mountain Lion

Page 17
Felis tigris
Tiger
Now *Panthera tigris*
Tiger

Page 18
Felis uncia
Snow-Leopard
Now *Uncia uncia*
Snow Leopard

Page 19
Felis onca
Jaguar
Now *Panthera onca*
Jaguar

Page 20
Felis pardus
Panther, or Leopard
Now *Panthera pardus*
Leopard

Page 21
Felis leopardus
Panther, or Leopard
Now *Panthera pardus*
Leopard

Page 22
Felis diardi
Clouded Tiger
Now *Neofelis nebulosa*
Clouded Leopard

Page 23
Felis marmorata
Little Marbled Tiger
Now *Pardofelis marmorata*
Marbled Cat

Page 24
Felis manul
Pallas's Thibetan Cat
Now *Otocolobus manul*
Pallas's Cat

Page 25
Felis pajeros
Pampas Cat
Now *Oncifelis colocolo*
Pampas Cat

Page 26
Felis colocolla
Molina's Guiana Cat
Now *Oreailurus jacobita*
Mountain Cat

Page 55
Felis caracal
Caracal
Now *Caracal caracal*
Caracal

Page 56
Felis domestica
Domestic Cat
Now *Felis catus*
Domestic Cat

Page 57
Cynailurus jubata
Cheetah, Hunting Leopard
Now *Acinonyx jubatus*
Cheetah

References

Baillie, Jonathan, and Brian Groombridge. 1996. 1996 IUCN red list of threatened animals. Gland (Switzerland) and Cambridge: International Union for Conservation of Nature and Natural Resources.

Wilson, Don E., and DeeAnn M. Reeder. 1993. Mammal species of the world: A taxonomic and geographic reference. Second edition. Washington and London: Smithsonian Institution Press.

Nowak, Ronald M. 1991. Walker's mammals of the world. Volume II. Fifth edition. Baltimore and London: The Johns Hopkins University Press.